What's the BUZZ?

Chase Buzz!

BEECH

PRAISE FOR
What's Your Buzz?

"No matter what industry or field you work in, *What's Your Buzz?* will give you simple insights to elevate your business. No matter how good your location, quality of product or services, it *always* comes down to people. To build strong teams, you must share the vision and use simple principles within a structure that everyone can easily understand. Steve's book will take you there."

—*Ron Wallace, Former President of UPS International, Author of* Leadership Lessons from a UPS Driver *and* Power of the Campaign Pyramid, *CEO of The Number One Group Entertainment*

"Steve has taken his great presentation style and put the concepts in a format for personal development. This book provides the tools to grow your business or climb the corporate ladder! All you have to do is follow the steps and change your BUZZ!"

—Vince Green, Field Sales Leader, Allstate

"If there was a PhD program for creating positive buzz, Steve Beecham could teach it. He comes to the top of my mind when thinking about someone in his profession, someone who cares about the community, and a motivational speaker. This man has MAJOR buzz!"

—Michael A. Pitcher, Former President and CEO,
LeasePlan USA

"For the past six-plus years, Steve has volunteered his time to run a workshop at RUMC Job Networking in Roswell, Georgia. Steve shares his 'buzz' strategies with professionals in career transition, and he demonstrates it too! Job seekers leave his workshop with exciting ideas they can immediately put into action. Steve even connects people to his friends to 'supercharge' their own personal networking activity. Steve may be the 'Straight Shooter' of the mortgage industry, but he is so much more. His 'buzz' has helped thousands of people get jobs. How many people can say that?"

—*Jay Litton, Volunteer Leader, RUMC Job Networking, Sales Director, MapR Technologies*

"Steve's first book, *Bass-Ackward Business*, is packed with wisdom—my entire team read and uses his approach. *What's Your Buzz?* builds on the foundation laid by *Bass-Ackward Business*. It's an excellent guidebook with practical steps that help you find, create, and share your buzz so you can grow your business."

—*Tony Rushin, Vice President of Sales and Marketing, Network 1 Consulting*

What's Your BUZZ?

Finding and Creating the Right Talk about You and Your Business

STEVE BEECHAM

BOOKLOGIX®
Alpharetta, GA

ISBN: 978-1-61005-716-5
Library of Congress Control Number: 2015920030

10 9 8 7 6 5 4 3 2   0 4 0 5 1 7

Printed in the United States of America

∞This paper meets the requirements of ANSI/NISO Z39.48-1992 (Permanence of Paper)

Cover Design by jGribble/INDUSTRY

A special thanks to Brian Hatch, who has been there for me since our Little League days and whose help and wisdom made this book a reality.

Getting people's money is easy once you have persuaded them to give you their time. Win the time of the people and their money will follow.

— ROY H. WILLIAMS
Author of *The Wizard of Ads: Turning Words into Magic and Dreamers into Millionaires*

CONTENTS

Introduction
WHAT IS BUZZ?

Life is pretty much a selling job. Whether we succeed or fail is largely a matter of how well we motivate the human beings with whom we deal to buy us and what we have to offer.

Success or failure in this job is essentially a matter of human relationships. It is a matter of the kind of reaction to us by our family members, customers, employees, employers, and fellow workers and associates. If this reaction is favorable we are quite likely to succeed. If the reaction is unfavorable we are doomed.

– ROBERT WOODRUFF
President of Coca-Cola, 1923–1954

People love to talk about each other; it's human nature. And if you're a small-business owner or salesperson trying to gain more business, your main drive should be getting people talking about you or your company. But how do you accomplish this?

One Word: BUZZ

Buzz is the word of mouth about you or your company that's out on the street, what people say about you to their friends and family or in reviews online. It is the thing that makes you **SIZZLE** and makes others want to spread the word about you.

Buzz is a noun—what you say about yourself when asked—and a verb—talking about yourself on the street.

What if I told you that you could control your buzz? Spin it from negative to positive? Or turn your nonexistent buzz into the word that's on the tip of everyone's tongue?

In a world where word of mouth sells more than any other type of marketing or advertising, you want the word in people's mouths to be a referral for you or your company. Per the Promotion Marketing Association, 48 percent of people asked said word of mouth was their top influencer for making a buying decision versus 27 percent for advertising. As you can see, buzz influences a large number of your referrals. If you have good buzz, let's face it—you probably wouldn't be reading this book. But if you have bad buzz or don't even know what your buzz is, it can make or break your referral business.

I once had a financial advisor who was one of the top-producing employees out of twelve thousand financial advisors working for a large company. He was in the top 5 or 10 percent, and was the biggest producer in his state. With this in mind, it came as a huge shock to him that his customer surveys were some of the worst scores out of everyone in the company. After hearing me speak about buzz, he called and asked me for help. I agreed, and after he officially hired me, off I drove to meet him for dinner. While having dinner with him, the reason for this guy's problem hit me almost immediately. I knew what he was doing wrong. I mean, I already knew what his problem was just from sitting with him! He just came across as a guy that people would find offensive. He was very full of himself— everything was all about him. The next morning, I went to his office and laid it out for him: "Dude, I've just got this sense that you've got some bad buzz. There's a reason why your customer-service scores are so low." But I needed to show him. He had two assistants who worked for him that shared the same office. I brought him over, sat down with them, and asked, "Ladies, when you're out around town and you tell people that you work for him, what do they say?"

His assistants both looked away. They wouldn't look us in the eye. It was obvious that it was bad enough that they weren't going to tell him. I suggested he call his wife right then and there and put her on speakerphone. He called her and said, "Hey, honey, I'm here with Beech and we're talking about my buzz, and he wanted me to call you. When you tell people in town that you're married to me, what do they say?"

She replied, "Oh, everybody in town knows you're a jerk."

After hearing this, he looked at his assistants and they nodded, adding, "But we tell them you're a nice jerk."

I watched a grown man cry. He had no clue.

This was a case of bad buzz. The good news is, even bad buzz can be turned into good buzz, and that's what this book is about.

No matter your buzz, once you take control of it, you have the power to change the way people think about you and your business.

Unfortunately, if you don't know what your buzz is, you can be losing referrals without even knowing it. Buzz is a way for you to gain a competitive edge.

There are three different types of buzz:
GOOD BUZZ,
BAD BUZZ,
AND NO BUZZ.

If you have **BAD BUZZ**, like the example above, you need to resolve it quickly and find a way to change it—or **SPIN IT**, as they say in the media—in order to gain more business. Bad buzz may leave a lasting impression, but not in the right way. With good buzz, you may think you're golden and no further work is needed, but you do need to find ways to mention, or **DRIP IT**, to others so that they become the ones doing the buzzing for you. Good buzz sets you apart in what it is you do from a business standpoint.

If I say, "This is my friend Paul. He is one of the top financial advisors in his company. Matter of fact, he is in the top one percent of the twelve thousand financial advisors that work for his firm. I remember when he first started. He would go door to door meeting people, telling them the story about his dad and uncle who were physicians and ended up broke because they were given bad financial advice, and he vowed to make sure others didn't end up the same way." Now that's **GOOD BUZZ**, but if no one is telling that story to others, then you won't remember him. You need other people (customers, friends, and neighbors) out there telling others why they should use you and not someone else.

Finally, if you have no buzz, you need to create some and get it out there. If I introduce you to Paul with, "This is my friend Paul. He's my neighbor," it doesn't set him apart or leave a lasting impression with anyone. There's no **BUZZ** about Paul. He is nobody special! It boils down to this: there needs to be something out there about you other than you're a "financial advisor." Your peers need to be telling people reasons *why* they think you are somebody others need to deal with. Ultimately, good buzz will lead to more referral business.

This is buzz, and it enhances the chance of someone calling on you for business.

Once you know what your buzz is, you've got to **COMMUNICATE YOUR BUZZ**. You've got to communicate to people about what you're doing. If someone is going to refer somebody to you, first they need to tell them *about* you. You need to educate them on why you're special or unique—a.k.a. your buzz—or you're leaving it up to them to fill in the blanks, which can be good or bad depending on what they say. Just know that if you're not putting your own buzz out there, others will do it for you.

Buzz is primarily about word of mouth. People are going to do business with those they know or trust, and if they don't know anyone in that business, they will seek referrals from their friends and family. It's a fact.

> **ULTIMATELY, GOOD BUZZ WILL LEAD TO MORE REFERRAL BUSINESS.**

WORD-OF-MOUTH STATISTICS

- More than 50 percent of the people who are going to make a purchase are going to try to find other people's opinions before they make that purchase.[1]

- A Planet Feedback Poll said that 61 percent of consumers trusted word of mouth.[2]

- According to a study by Maritz Marketing Research, 70 percent of us rely on the advice of others when selecting a new doctor.[3] (My own dad—a physician—called me and asked me who my doctor was. He was looking for a new doctor!)

- 53 percent of moviegoers rely on someone else's advice about a movie choice.[4]

- 43 percent of us use the advice of friends for information about flights, hotels, or rental cars before making any decisions.[5]

- David Reddick, a well-known C-level recruiter from Atlanta, says 50 percent of the people who get hired do so because of a friend or acquaintance. Somebody knows someone looking for a job and connects the job seeker with the employer.

As consumers, we trust word of mouth more than the companies or individuals we are seeking because we know a company is only going to have great things to say about their business, or highlight only the positive things people are saying about them. So, how can you tap into what people are already telling others about you? Better yet, how can you control what people are saying?

This is the ultimate goal. Once you discover, define, and refine your buzz, you'll be ready to communicate it to others. This will create good buzz for yourself or your company, thus elevating your status, or what I like to call **GOING PRO**. Every client wants to deal with the rock star in that field, right? In your community, you want to be known as the go-to person for what you do, because there are very few situations where you're the only option. There's always competition, so it's paramount that you separate yourself from the competition. If you get your buzz out there, and it's more positive, catchy, and memorable, or **BUZZABLE,** than anyone else's, that's when you'll gain more referral business and make more money.

Part One

DISCOVERING BUZZ

1

The Different TYPES OF BUZZ

Educators take something simple and make it complicated. Communicators take something complicated and make it simple.

— JOHN C. MAXWELL

People are going to talk about you and your business; there's no escaping it. The power to control what they say, however, is entirely in your hands. How? By controlling your buzz, or the word of mouth about you or your company that's out on the street.

There are three different types of buzz:

① **PERSONAL BUZZ** *(opinions of you as an individual)*

② **PROFESSIONAL BUZZ** *(opinions of you as a business professional)*

③ **CORPORATE BUZZ** *(opinions of your company from both your employees and customers)*

This chapter details the importance of all three and how to uncover yours, an important task when remembering that the ultimate goal with the use of buzz is to get more referral business.

PERSONAL BUZZ

When I started out in the mortgage business, I figured I would do well because a lot of my friends from high school had moms who were real-estate agents. I thought I could just go visit them and they would send me business, because I had pretty much known them most of my life.

But a funny thing happened: they didn't send me any business. Zilch! I did my best to cater to them. I would buy them lunch or bring donuts to their office. I would pay for advertising for the houses they had listed. And yet, I got nothing. Eventually, I gave up on courting them and started to pick up business from agents with whom I didn't have long-term relationships.

Later on, as my confidence grew and I became a better mortgage broker, I decided I needed to know why they had never sent me any business. After all, they had known me most of my life, and the fact that they didn't seem to want to help me out was troubling. I finally asked an agent friend who shared an office with a few of the moms to help me uncover the truth. Come to find out, I had some **BAD PERSONAL BUZZ**.

She told me the reason they wouldn't send me business was because they remembered me as a "wild and crazy guy" in high school. They had heard stories from their kids that I had a carefree spirit, and they didn't want to give their good clients to a wild man.

As demonstrated, your personal buzz is about more than just who you are as a salesperson or employee for a company. It's about your reputation, personality, and character—who you are as an individual, or at least, who people *think* you are. Your personal buzz is all about you as an individual, outside work. If you're looking for more referral business for your company or professional career, there's a chance that your personal buzz can get in the way of your professional buzz.

Now if you're a business owner looking to bring on salespeople to represent your company to the public, you need to be aware of these individuals' personal buzz. Careful interviewing, diligent hiring practices, and calling for character references can help you filter through candidates and eliminate those who have bad personal buzz—but you shouldn't disqualify someone just because of this, as long as you have a plan to **SPIN** that bad personal buzz in the process to highlight their professional buzz instead.

Although having bad personal buzz is the most obvious obstacle to overcome, having good personal buzz can also be a hindrance—if it doesn't tie in to your professional life.

At a meeting with some financial advisors, I picked one of the people in attendance and asked him to stand up. I then asked everyone in the room to tell me only the good things they knew about this man. The comments were things like, "He is a good father," "He used to be a great basketball player," and "He is a good man who spends lots of time with his family."

All of these comments seemed well and good, until I asked the gentleman if those same comments would get him any financial business. Nobody had said anything about his business acumen; nothing about how he made money for his customers, enjoyed helping young families plan for retirement, or that he helped little, old ladies with their finances after their husbands died. No one said anything about him being a great salesperson or a top performer for the company they all worked for. No one said he was exceptional in trading stocks or selling bonds and annuities. I asked him if that was what he thought they would say, and his answer was no. I asked him if the responses he received would make a potential customer seek him out to manage their money, and once again, he said no.

Wondering what those comments *did* qualify him for, one of the other participants in the room said, "Youth basketball coach!"

"Now you may understand why you don't have some of the customers you would like to have," I noted. "People in your community know you as a great dad and basketball player, but not as a great financial advisor."

The bottom line is this: your **PERSONAL BUZZ** is critical to your **PROFESSIONAL SUCCESS**. People will pay extra to deal with a professional, so if they only hear personal buzz about you that doesn't relate at all to your business, or that is even worse—damaging—it can hurt your referral business.

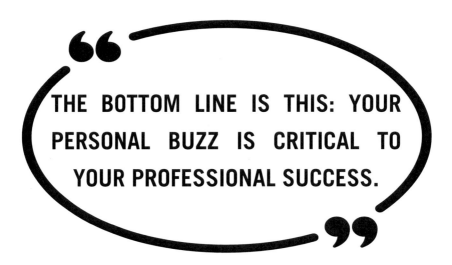

> **THE BOTTOM LINE IS THIS: YOUR PERSONAL BUZZ IS CRITICAL TO YOUR PROFESSIONAL SUCCESS.**

PROFESSIONAL BUZZ

As a small-business owner, you have salespeople working for you who communicate directly with your clients. Ultimately, how the clients perceive these salespeople will affect your corporate buzz, or the overall opinion of your actual business.

Professional buzz refers to the opinions people, including those at your company, have of you as a business professional.

The company has to build trust with the client, and that starts with the salesperson who is representing the company. So what is that person's professional buzz? Do they always make sure the customer is taken care of?

Do they never return phone calls in a timely manner? A salesperson's professional buzz can make or break a referral. Remember the story of the financial advisor who was labeled a jerk? Being a jerk was his professional buzz, because he was cocky and arrogant in all of his business dealings. His clients were focusing on the negative aspects of doing business with him, rather than focusing on how much money he could make them.

CORPORATE BUZZ

When you own a company, you need to not only consider your personal buzz about you as an individual and your professional buzz about you as a business person, but also the buzz about your company, i.e., your **CORPORATE BUZZ**. Your corporate buzz is made up of employee buzz and customer buzz, or the opinions of both the employees and customers about the company.

Both are critical to the success of your organization. Once you know that buzz, you can use it to help change the work culture and better accomplish your goals as a company. Corporate buzz is critical because it is not only about you, but your employees too.

Sometimes the salesperson is the same person who owns and runs the business. Think of an attorney who owns their own firm. In this case, the professional buzz and the corporate buzz are one and the same, because the owner and the company are inextricably tied together.

An example would be my friend Don. I might **BUZZ** you on him with the following: "You need to meet my friend Don. He is the best zoning attorney around, and I think he could really help you with the City of Alpharetta on your project. He knows more than anybody about the kind of variances they would allow. His firm Smith & Smith has been doing real-estate law for years."

There are two parts to corporate buzz:
EMPLOYEE BUZZ
CUSTOMER BUZZ

EMPLOYEE BUZZ

Your employee buzz is twofold: There is the internal employee buzz, what they are saying about the company, and then the actual buzz being put out there about the individuals representing the company. Internal employee buzz is important to consider when trying to keep everyone going in the right direction. Think of the workplace as a wagon that's going somewhere. You have an end goal, a destination you're trying to reach, and a team to drive the wagon. To get where you want to go, everyone on the team needs to push or pull the wagon.

However, when your company's employee buzz isn't clear, you may have people who are just tagging along for the ride. They're not taking concrete steps to send a

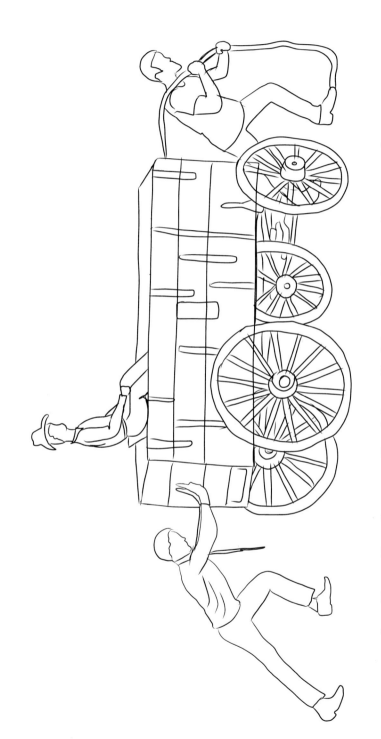

Are Your Employees Pushing, Pulling, or Along for the Ride?

message about your company or improve the company's buzz. Instead, they're sitting on top of the wagon, adding to the weight of the load and slowing down the process. This is not always because they're a bad employee, but because the management is not relating to the core workers why improving the company's buzz is such an initiative. When everybody is on the same page with a clear message and service they're aiming to achieve through the company, then everybody is pushing or pulling the wagon.

Most employees are in the dark about the direction of the company and do not understand why the leader makes certain decisions. Part of what makes your corporate buzz what it is, is a lot of people are in the cold as to what the boss is doing. As a leader or owner of the company, you need to explain to people why you're going in a certain direction. That way, when employees talk amongst themselves, they understand why they're going in that direction instead of guessing aimlessly.

*The fate of your company is in the hands of
your people. Train them well.*

—ROY H. WILLIAMS
Author of *The Wizard of Ads:
Turning Words into Magic and Dreamers
into Millionaires*

**YOUR CORPORATE BUZZ IS MADE UP
OF EMPLOYEE BUZZ AND CUSTOMER
BUZZ, OR THE OPINIONS OF BOTH THE
EMPLOYEES AND CUSTOMERS ABOUT
THE COMPANY.**

REAL-LIFE EMPLOYEE BUZZ

I'm coaching an attorney firm on growing and maintaining their buzz. There are three partners, and there are four juniors who want to be partners one day. They're all great attorneys who do a lot of work, but the partners are starting to realize that the juniors are not bringing in any business. While working with the juniors, I asked them straight out, "Why aren't you bringing in any business?" They told me that they were trying.

My next question was, "What happens if you don't?"

"Nothing."

This was the fundamental problem: nothing happened when they didn't bring in any business. The partners at the top hadn't relayed to the juniors what was expected of them and what would happen if those expectations weren't met.

The top partners *should* have told the juniors, "You don't have to bring in any business today, but if you're going to stay with us long term and help us develop, you need to bring in business. If you can't bring any business, you can't stay."

Another aspect to employee buzz is what people are out there saying about the company and the individuals who make up the company. When people are out there **BUZZING** about your company, they have to convince people to use not only your company, but also the people working for your company. As the company, you've got to give them the information they need to not only brag about the company, but to also brag about the individual employees, because that is who the customer will be calling and talking to. You must have buzz about both your company and your employees. Keeping your employees informed and setting clear expectations will help keep them invested in the company and its success.

> **"IF YOU GET ALL OF YOUR EMPLOYEES ON THE SAME PAGE SO THAT EVERYONE IS SENDING THE SAME MESSAGE OF WHAT YOU WANT PEOPLE TO KNOW ABOUT YOUR COMPANY, THE PROCESS OF CHANGING THE CORPORATE BUZZ WILL BE AFFECTED POSITIVELY."**

Along these same lines, your employees need to talk about the company in the same way when they are outside of work. I am currently coaching a New York City-based company that is working as a unit to bolster the buzz of the company. I advised the business owner to talk to all the salespeople and ask how most people described their company. Amongst these twenty or thirty people, they needed to come up with a common way to describe the company, so that everyone would talk about the company in the same manner. This way, if your employees are out and about and someone asks them what they do, they can appropriately respond with the right buzz about the company.

"YOU MUST HAVE BUZZ ABOUT BOTH YOUR COMPANY AND YOUR EMPLOYEES."

Let's say that I have two secretaries and I'm an insurance agent. I sit down with them and explain that we must try to get our buzz out there a little bit better, so we need to talk about how we communicate our buzz. We need to make a list about what we think is great about not only me, but also the insurance agency and the secretaries as individuals— the time they put into the business, the amount of knowledge they have, and how they go above and beyond for customer service. This is all so we can develop some strategies around how we talk about each other and make sure we're all saying the same thing.

If you get all of your employees on the same page so that everyone is sending the same message of what you want people to know about your company, the process of changing the corporate buzz will be affected positively.

An example would be meeting a new mom at the soccer field. The new mom may ask, "Where do you work?"

Your employee could ideally say something like this: "I work for Patrick Smith Insurance. We are a top-one-hundred office. I don't know of another agent in town who has the years of experience in their office as we do. You have to be the best to work for Patrick, and you have to pass his 'desire to be helpful' test."

Finding YOUR BUZZ

People get great pleasure from offering help and knowing they can be called upon as a source of reliable information.

–DANA RILEY

F inding your buzz is all about seeking information from those who have already done business with you, and even more so, those who *haven't* done business with you. If you have **BAD BUZZ**, you will most likely find this out from those who didn't do business with you. If you have **GOOD BUZZ**, it can come back to you in a multitude of ways, including the simplest approach: someone comes up to you and literally says, "I hear ___ about ___!" For instance, they might say to me, "I hear they call you the Straight Shooter because you always tell your clients the truth!"

When you're trying to find your buzz, make sure you talk to both camps—people who know and like you, and those who you haven't done business with.

If good buzz doesn't come back to you, then the most obvious sign is that you have bad buzz. If the bad buzz comes back to you, then your house is on fire, so to speak. You must immediately make efforts to put out that fire, or it will only get worse. Considering that most people don't like giving others bad news, if you're hearing the bad buzz, then you've got a significant problem. You must be mature enough to step back and consider why they're telling you these things. The truth is, they're telling you because there is a problem, and you must address it. The ultimate goal is to hear your good buzz come back to you.

BUZZ SURVEYS

How do you know if you're putting wrong or inappropriate buzz out there? If you find yourself asking this question, then you need to do a buzz survey. Whether you're getting positive, negative, or zero feedback already, answers like, "I met him through my son, and I have never used him because I don't think I can trust him because of how wild he was when he was younger." Crushed again! But the people who didn't know my backstory, used my services, and liked me came back with, "I met him from a mutual customer, and I use him because he is a straight shooter." What a difference from no trust to high trust! "Straight shooter" turned out to be the most-often-used phrase from participants in my survey—an important facet to look out for in your own surveys that we will discuss further in Part Two: Define and Refine Your Buzz.

It's important to get an outsider to do the survey for you because people are going to talk more frankly if they feel it's off the record. To find out your true buzz, you must create an "off the record" atmosphere for the person you are surveying. This is the best way for them to give you true, honest feedback. This is especially true when trying to discover your interoffice buzz.

When doing a buzz survey, people will always reveal the negative before pointing out the positive. For that reason, it's important to have raving fans in the mix with people who decided not to do business with you. This way, you can better understand your good buzz and bad buzz.

I was once asked to do a buzz survey on a president of a bank that went under. A lot of people had invested in the bank, so a lot of his friends and fellow civilians lost a lot of money. He got a job as president of another bank in town, but he soon realized he was getting the cold shoulder from the local residents. Believing he must have bad buzz, he brought me on to implement a buzz survey. First, we sat down and figured out the questions we wanted to ask, making sure the questions would be **BUZZABLE**, or memorable. We mentioned in the survey that a lot of banks had gone under during that time. With this fact in mind, those surveyed didn't immediately think of my client as the bad guy. In actuality, the buzz survey results revealed that the "cold shoulder" treatment was actually due to his *customers* feeling inadequate because of their own businesses failing, and they did not want him to know. His perception of what people thought of him wasn't 100 percent accurate, after all.

If you're having trouble coming up with buzzable questions in your own survey, you can reference the survey in the back of the book.

Once you're ready to do your own buzz survey, you will need to make a list of friends, past customers, current customers, and potential customers who *should* be doing business with you. The more people who know you that you can involve with the survey, the better. Likewise, the more people who have done business with you, the better. It is also important to hire someone to administer the survey who has not yet met the survey participants. This way, the participants' answers won't run a chance of being biased based on who they're talking to.

Have your survey administrator call and follow a set prompt: "We are doing an informational survey on [your name or company] to help them determine what they are doing right and what they may want to consider changing."

You'll then want the survey administrator to ask the same questions to each survey taker to get consistent answers. Remember, have your administrator ready to respond to the survey takers' answers with some good buzz about you. This is what I refer to as **DRIPPING**. Seize every opportunity to get your good buzz out there—especially in your buzz surveys!

O T H E R   W A Y S   T O
F I N D   Y O U R   B U Z Z

Another way to find your buzz is to "shop" for yourself. Pretend you aren't you, and ask people you don't know in the community about your business. For example, I might ask my waitress at a restaurant or someone at the community fair, "Have you heard of Steve Beecham? I'm looking to refinance my house, and I was wondering what you know about him." This is a great, quick, easy way to understand your buzz. You just have to make sure the person you're talking to really doesn't know you. If the prospect of approaching strangers to talk about yourself is too scary for you introverts out there, ask a friend or family member to do it. They could easily ask their dry cleaner or bartender if they know of any great mortgage broker (or whatever your business may be), then nonchalantly mention your name.

One of the first steps in learning about your buzz is to start listening to how people introduce you.

If someone simply introduces me as a mortgage broker, that indicates that I may not have any buzz, because there are plenty of mortgage brokers around. What sets me apart? If they say, "He's a mortgage broker but he has a **WILD PAST**, so you might not want to trust him with your higher clientele," I have **BAD BUZZ. GOOD BUZZ** would be the following: "I want you to meet Steve. He's the guy that knows everybody around here. They call him the **MAYOR OF ALPHARETTA**, and he's one of the **TOP MORTGAGE GUYS IN TOWN**." He said I'm one of the best mortgage guys around, so I'll **TAKE THAT BUZZ**. Now when I talk to people, I want to emphasize that I'm one of the best mortgage guys in town. "Hi, I'm Steve," I can say. "I like to think I'm one of the best mortgage guys around. I was fortunate to be rated by the *Atlanta Business Chronicle* as one of the top mortgage brokers in town." I'm acknowledging the buzz that's already out there, as well as **DRIPPING BUZZ** to that person.

In the latter case, my friend **DRIPPED**—i.e., mentioned— some pretty good buzz: that I'm one of the best mortgage guys in town. But let's say my friend introduced me this way: "This is my buddy Steve. They call him the mayor of Alpharetta."

This is still good, but it doesn't quite do the trick. If someone is in need of a loan, then the buzz that I'm "the mayor of Alpharetta" may not mean much to them. Sure, it may indicate that I know a lot of people or a lot of people know me, but it says nothing about my ability as a mortgage broker.

Once you discover your good buzz, make efforts to communicate it **(DRIP IT)** to others. It's important to have buzz that will be considered good across all platforms and not require extensive explanation or thought.

DRIPPING: Effectively communicating good buzz about yourself or your company to others in conversation in such a way that doesn't sound like bragging.

Part Two

DEFINE AND REFINE YOUR BUZZ

3

Shape Your OWN BUZZ

Making the unknown known to others increases the opportunity for them to like you and admire you.

—PATTI WOOD

Now you know what your buzz is—the good, bad, ugly, or nonexistent. You've done your buzz surveys, you've talked to people, but now you must take a step back and look at everything. The next step is to analyze the patterns you see and ask yourself, Is that the proper buzz? Is that the buzz that I want out there?

DEFINING YOUR BUZZ

Once you've done your survey and you have all the feedback and information you need, it's time to analyze the results and find the pattern. In some surveys, you'll see feedback like **"GREAT," "FANTASTIC," or "EXCELLENT."** It's not the same word, but they're saying positive things about you. If a lot of people said my knowledge is **DEEP, GREAT, AND EXTENSIVE,** I have to take a step back and figure out how I want to describe my knowledge. I'm now in charge of figuring out what I want people to say about me.

I might take the concept of what they're saying and refine it a little bit. I'd say that my knowledge on mortgages is so great that I'm essentially the "Doctor of Mortgage-ology" because I have a lot of experience, twenty years in the industry, and extensive education on the subject, like a Phd in finance. While "great" or "deep" may not be very **BUZZWORTHY**, "Doctor of Mortgage-ology" certainly is! With this in mind, I would decide that I need to use this phrase when talking to people and describing myself. When someone asks me what makes me special, I can say, "My friends actually call me the 'Doctor of Mortgage-ology' because for the past twenty years, I have dedicated myself to being a student of the subject and have learned everything there is to know about mortgages. I basically have a PhD!" If I start to say "Doctor of Mortgage-ology" repeatedly, that becomes my **BUZZABLE PHRASE**. Now people will know I have deep, extensive knowledge in my profession.

When I did my first buzz survey, I wanted to find out the qualities I needed in order to work successfully with real-estate agents. This was important because seven out of ten agents said they would work with a new loan officer, even though 80 percent were currently using a loan officer they had worked with before. I used this survey to understand how to acquire new agents and become "one of the top-five mortgage brokers in the state of Georgia," which I would eventually become. With that, **I JUST BUZZED YOU!**

From the survey, I learned that several different people thought of me as a "straight shooter." They said things like, "He shoots me straight about whether I will be able to afford a new house." So, here was my **BUZZABLE PHRASE**. I started using "straight shooter" as my buzz, or personal brand. I adopted the slogan **"THE STRAIGHT SHOOTER"** as a way to buzz my trustworthiness. I put this slogan on fliers, newsletters, and the business cards I handed out to agents. Every time I had a chance, I let them know I was a **STRAIGHT SHOOTER**, because I would always tell them up front what their customer's chances were of qualifying for a house.

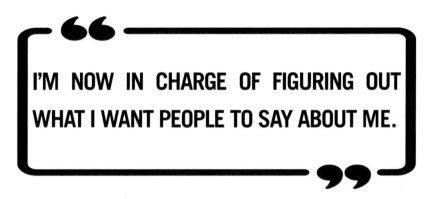

"
I'M NOW IN CHARGE OF FIGURING OUT WHAT I WANT PEOPLE TO SAY ABOUT ME.
"

CREATING MEMORABLE BUZZ

When you finally decide on what message you want to send as a company or businessperson, you need to make sure that message is **BUZZABLE**, or **BUZZWORTHY.**

How do you know what's buzzable? Simply put: it's worth remembering.

To create memorable buzz, it all comes down to the words you choose to deliver your buzz. In order to truly understand the importance of the words, phrases, or stories you choose, you first have to understand how the brain receives and processes the buzz, and then most importantly, how it decides whether or not your buzz is memorable— worth committing to memory.

Memorable buzz is just like gossip; it simply **rolls** off your tongue. But why? What is it about that "juicy" piece of gossip that drives our urge to share it? Psychologist C. Buf Myer best describes this in her article "The Urge to Gossip." She explains that gossip starts with a message or piece of information that we find shocking, or more aptly put, unexpected, which then triggers an emotional reaction. She takes this one step further, explaining that "emotions trigger 'action tendencies' (like fight or flight), including an urge to communicate."[6] **GOSSIP AND BUZZ ARE ONE AND THE SAME AND CAN ALMOST BE USED INTERCHANGEABLY.** Both create excitement or stimulus—the emotional trigger that leads us to repeat what we just heard.

Roy H. Williams examines this concept even further in his book *Secret Formulas of the Wizard of Ads*. He identifies the different parts of the brain that deal with how information is received, processed, and hopefully committed to memory—which is the whole point of this conversation. You want your customer to commit the message you are sending to memory in hopes that in the future, they will repeat this message to others.

However, not all messages received are committed to memory. Some are rejected. So how do you make your message stick like glue? It all starts with the words you choose. Your buzz has to be **CATCHY**. You need to find that one word or phrase that **CATCHES FIRE AND RATTLES THE BRAIN**. A good example is **"NEVER RATTLES."** When speaking to others, you need to say over and over, "Nothing rattles me," and "I don't get rattled easily." Because these words are so catchy, they will catch your listener's attention and they will commit them to memory, especially if you use these words frequently when talking about yourself.

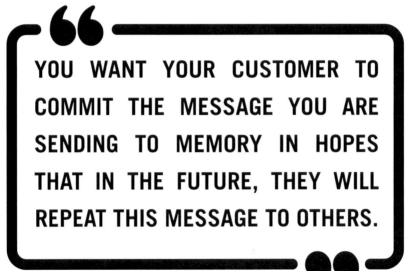

> YOU WANT YOUR CUSTOMER TO COMMIT THE MESSAGE YOU ARE SENDING TO MEMORY IN HOPES THAT IN THE FUTURE, THEY WILL REPEAT THIS MESSAGE TO OTHERS.

Likewise, the way you phrase your buzz is as important as the words you choose. **YOU MUST MAKE SURE THAT IT'S SOMETHING CATCHY THAT PEOPLE WILL REMEMBER.** A generic phrase like "we have great customer service" or "competitive pricing" is not really buzzable. Just as "never rattles" is a buzzable phrase, so is "gets it done" and "lightning fast." Williams adds to this, advising:

Pay close attention to your action words, your verbs. Listeners can take no action they have not first imagined. To cause them to imagine an action, you must use a verb. But never one they were expecting.[7]

If you want your buzz to stick, you must first understand how your buzz is received by the brain, processed, and then hopefully committed to memory, which will better help you to understand the importance of the words, phrases, and most importantly, verbs you use. Next is getting those words and phrases past the "goalie" of the brain: the Broca.

In order to get people to communicate your buzz, we need to trigger an emotional reaction, as Dr. Myer stated. These emotional reactions go down in the prefrontal cortex, which Williams describes as "the seat of emotion, planning, and judgement." Once the emotional reaction is triggered, action tendencies will shortly follow, and the area of the brain responsible for action is the motor association cortex. **THIS IS WHERE THE MAGIC HAPPENS,** and actions taken are that individual telling everyone in town why they must come see you. This is your goal, and all you have to do is kick that buzz right into the net. But be strategic with the words you choose, because if they don't pack a punch and aren't catchy, shocking, or unexpected, then the Broca area of your brain will quickly block your message from ever entering the goal. Williams goes on to say, "Verbs will move your message past Broca's Area, that part of the brain that rejects the mundane and ignores the predictable, but allows the delightfully surprising to have immediate access to the motor association cortex."

Now that you have an understanding of the importance of choosing catchy words, you'll also want to make sure that the buzz you put out there for yourself correlates with the existing buzz people are already saying about you or your business. If your buzz survey shows the same phrase showing up over and over, then that buzz is already there. You don't have to change it; you just need to **TURBOCHARGE** it. Start using that phrase often to talk about yourself, so that you're basically saying you agree with it. The phrase will then spread faster because everyone already understands it. If it needs a little tune-up, then take it upon yourself to refine it specifically to your goal, and start dripping that message out to people. Then they can correct themselves and say, "Oh, that's the way I should say it." Eventually, it will catch on, but it takes repetition. Jane Fonda put it best when she said, "We cannot always control our thoughts, but we can control our words, and repetition impresses the subconscious, and we are then master of the situation."

Another way to buzz is through storytelling. If you can't decide what's buzzable about you, then there may be a certain story that you tell that becomes your **BUZZABLE STORY**. It's really the easiest, quickest way to start getting your buzz out, because people will always remember a good story. Just note that it needs to be a real story, and keep it short. That way, when someone is telling someone about you, they can retell that story with ease. For instance, should someone ask me how the mortgage business is going, I can reply with: "Great. I have really been working the millennials. You know, I love having them come in so I can explain the mortgage process to them. It's sort of like a Mortgage 101 class. Afterward, they all say, 'I wish they had taught this in school! Thank you, Mr. Beecham, for making this easy to understand.' So if you know anyone who needs a Mortgage 101 class, let me know!" This memorable story filled with catchy words and phrases is bound to be repeated should the listener be in a conversation about mortgages.

Bottom line: what's valuable to your listener is what sticks with them long after the conversation is over. Whether it's a catchy phrase, an interesting fact, or a great story, your listener is more apt to retain that information you give them if you deliver your buzz with passion and authenticity. The more passionate you are about your buzz, the more likely your listener is to remember it—and pass on that information to others. Passion is buzzable, and at the end of the day, that's what all consumers are looking for: a business with passion and dedication to their work.

> **BOTTOM LINE: WHAT'S VALUABLE TO YOUR LISTENER IS WHAT STICKS WITH THEM LONG AFTER THE CONVERSATION IS OVER.**

Part Three

COMMUNICATE YOUR BUZZ

It's All in Your DELIVERY

I've always been in the right place and time. Of course, I steered myself there.

—BOB HOPE

Once you have identified your buzz, analyzed it, and redefined it into **BUZZABLE BUZZ**, it's time to deliver it. You can deliver buzz in one of four ways:

DRIP IT—Mention your buzz in small, bite-sized pieces.

SPIN IT—Turn your bad buzz into good buzz through providing another interpretation.

DUMP IT—Unload *all* of your buzz at once.

CREATE IT—Reference your personal history or backstory as a source of buzz.

The type of buzz your survey came back with will determine what you decide to do with it and how you communicate your buzz moving forward.

D R I P P I N G   Y O U R   B U Z Z

Simply put, dripping is getting out what's cool about yourself by leaking droplets of your buzz.

You can drip your buzz into conversation, during buzz surveys, or even in your e-mail signature. The goal is to drip with the natural flow of conversation, finding natural opportunities to sneak in the good word about yourself without having braggadocio or turning the faucet on at full force and giving too much information.

When I go up to speak, people don't always have background information on me. The person who hired me may not have told the audience much about me, so they have a limited understanding of my background. They probably wonder, *Who is this guy who says he can tell us all this?* Even if I have a bio up online, that's all they have to go on. So, when I go up there, it would be prudent for me to drip them with stuff about me to "set the table," so to speak. As I speak, I drip in things about me that will lead the audience to understand I know what I'm talking about.

It's important to know when to drip, and to know the difference between dripping and bragging. You've got to see an opening to drip; otherwise you're just gloating.

Once you are aware of your professional, or even personal buzz, you can start feeding this to clients, but first you must build trust with them. You should make the conversation about them first, not about you or the company. Ask questions, seek information, and find out what the customer is looking for, because keep in mind: it's all about them. It's natural for us to want to jump in, but your client will be turned off if you jump in to talk about yourself or your company when what he really wants is to talk about himself. So let him talk. What you will find is that 75 percent of the time, after you have let them talk about themselves, they will eventually ask about you and your company.

This is a **BUZZABLE MOMENT**. They have presented an opportunity for you to paint a picture of yourself and the company. This is an indicator that you have established the relationship. The secret is to wait until they have asked you, not during the time you are asking them questions. If you do that, you are only trying to one-up them or say to them, "I'm as good as you." Avoid this as much as you can. Using this technique is absolutely the best way to drip your professional buzz.

> *If you spend time learning about them, they will spend time learning about you—it works almost every time.*

Once the client has asked about you or your business, there are two components to the buzz that you give them. First, you need to drip buzz on why the company is one worth being with, i.e., the **CORPORATE BUZZ**. Second, you should drip buzz on why you are the best person to represent the company, i.e., your **PROFESSIONAL BUZZ**.

You can also drip awards or special recognitions that you have received—all without saying a word. For example, you go into an insurance agent's office and notice that he has multiple plaques on the wall. Although you may not walk around to investigate what each plaque says, you take note that he has multiple plaques, which implies excellence. Each one of those plaques is dripping buzz, because each implies a time where he did something significant. The takeaway of this example is this: Your customers need to know that you're highly successful, because we all want to do business with someone who knows their business like the back of their hand. However, after some time, your customer will not be coming to your office anymore. Thus, you need to create the same impression verbally.

To do this drip your achievements by casually working them into conversation. Take a financial advisor who just won a trip to London because he was in the top 1 percent of employees who sold life insurance in his company. He typically meets with his client Mrs. Smith every quarter, so he must explain why he is postponing their usual meet-up. Taking advantage of the situation, he tells her, "Mrs. Smith, I know we meet every quarter and our next meeting should be in June. I need to get with you on that. I'm going to be out of town the first half of June because I just won a trip to London—I was in the top one percent of all the people who sold life insurance at the company. I need to see you either before or after I go." This statement not only appeases his client, but drips that he is excelling in his business and that she should feel comfortable with him as her financial advisor because he is in the top 1 percent.

The success of dripping also depends upon your tone. It's important to buzz using the right tone and perspective. You have to seize the opportunity to mention it, but you can't use it as a way to be better than the person in front of you. You can't one-up the person in front of you with your buzz.

An additional way to drip successfully is when your competitor's upset client comes to you. Rather than launching into how horrible the other company is, you should focus on the client and their concerns that arose from the situation, asking them questions like, "What are the problems you're having there? What are the concerns?" The client has already told you they are leaving your competitor, so you don't need to sell yourself or the company. You just have to convince them that you will take care of their concerns. For example, if their concern is pricing, you should say, "Well, we pride ourselves on not being too expensive, but we don't want to be cheap and not give you the services. Most of the people we have done work for love our prices. Let me sit down with you and go over the price and alleviate your concern. Hopefully you will love our prices too." In that case, one of the things you are dripping them with is that your customers love your prices.

Just remember:

WHEN A PERSON ASKS YOU A QUESTION ABOUT SOMETHING YOU DO, AND THERE'S AN OPPORTUNITY FOR YOU TO ADD SOMETHING VALUABLE TO THAT, YOU NEED TO DRIP BUZZ TO THEM.

In the same manner, your employees should always keep in mind that there will be opportunities for them to drip buzz about you and your company. When asked what they do in a social setting, they could say, "Oh, I'm a paralegal for Mr. Smith. He's one of the best divorce attorneys in Atlanta. The *Atlanta Business Chronicle* says that he's one of the top-fifty divorce attorneys in the city. If you know anybody who needs a divorce, you might send them over to see him." Her employer dripped her with buzz, which she then dripped to a potential customer.

That's buzz, but it's not the main goal.

The main goal is for your friends and customers to have the information—to know that you're amazing at what you do—so that when they're in a setting and somebody is talking about you, they've got ammunition to tell that person why they need to call you and do business with you.

You want to be the guy that everybody calls when they have insurance problems, or legal problems, or whatever kind of problems your career deals with. That's what the main goal should be: getting good stuff about you out into the community.

Where dripping takes place is not as big of a deal as understanding that you will have lots of opportunities to drip exciting buzz about yourself to people. Everywhere you go, be ready to buzz others *when asked*. Again: you never want to buzz others without them asking first! You want them to be genuinely interested in your response so they are open to hearing the buzz.

S P I N N I N G   Y O U R   B U Z Z

Generally, businesses that have bad buzz act like they aren't interested in the buzz about them. But who are they kidding? If the buzz is bad, the business is bad, and this is something you need to address quickly. **YOU NEED TO SPIN YOUR BUZZ, OR TURN THAT BAD BUZZ INTO GOOD BUZZ NOT BY DENYING IT, BUT BY OFFERING A NEW INTERPRETATION.**

If there are four of us standing around at a cocktail party, and I can give you information that you don't have, it elevates my status and makes me feel good. It's easier to give negative information than it is to give positive information, and so people will naturally give negative information to increase their status. That is why it's even more important to address the bad buzz right away with a backstory that helps people understand why the bad buzz exists. Explain how you plan to change that, and then drip them with good buzz.

Let's go back to the story about my financial advisor whose buzz was that he was a jerk. After we discovered his bad buzz, we went back in his office. I told him that in order to spin the bad buzz into good buzz, he needed to tell me his story. He proceeded to tell me that he grew up on the wrong side of the tracks, his parents were very poor, and that when he got into high school and became the high school quarterback, it elevated his status in the community. He began receiving college scholarships, and eventually went on to college on a full-ride scholarship playing quarterback. He was the toast of the town. When he returned home after graduating, he talked to some of the people who were wealthy in town and started managing their money. Somewhere in that process, he became too cocky and too confident. And there it was: the root of his bad buzz. So how could we spin this?

He had an appointment that day, and I asked if I could sit in and observe. The plan was for him to do what he normally did: go through the client's money situation with them, tell them how they're doing, and so on. When he was finished, he was going to address the bad buzz and we were going to spin them some good buzz. But first, we had to *find* some good buzz. So, as planned, he spent an hour going over his client's business with them. At the end of the meeting, he acknowledged my presence and said, "Steve's here coaching me today, and I just found out that a lot of people in town think I'm a jerk."

This little old lady leans back in her chair and says, "You just found that out today? Everybody knows you are a jerk!"

I jumped in and asked, "Why do you all use him then?"

"Because he makes us money," she responded simply. "Everybody in town knows he makes you money." There it was! The positive buzz.

From that, we started to spin his bad buzz into good buzz. He had to address the bad buzz first, so from now on when he runs into anyone from town, he tells them, "A lot of people think I'm a jerk, but now I realize that I haven't been treating people right, especially people on the other side of the tracks who really have a problem with how I'm handling my success." Then he hits them with good buzz: "I've been so focused on making people money that I haven't really focused on how people view me in the community. I want to change that."

Once you find out your bad buzz, you must immediately find a way to explain or justify why that bad buzz is out there about you, and then you should provide them justification for the bad buzz.

Next, you should drip them with the good buzz that you have identified and refined from your buzz survey.

Another example of spinning bad buzz was when I did my first buzz survey and found out why all my friends' real-estate moms didn't want to do business with me. The answers shocked me. How could I build more trust with the moms and generate a better buzz from them?

One day while I was in the real-estate office, one of the moms was sitting at her desk crying. I walked over and asked her what the problem was. She told me her husband had just lost his job, and they weren't sure what they were going to do. I told her I was sorry and asked what kind of work he did. She told me, and I told her I was going to work on finding him a job right away. I told her that I knew she still viewed me as that kid her son knew in high school, but that I had become very successful by building relationships with others. I started calling all the people in town I knew that could possibly help him with a job. Several people instructed me to tell the man to give them a call. Lo and behold, he got a job, and shortly after that day, I got a call from that mom saying she had a customer for me. She wanted to show her thanks for what I did.

Instead of feeling defeated that these moms would never send me business, I confronted the problem and then helped in a different way. **THE BEST WAY TO REDUCE OR RID YOURSELF COMPLETELY OF BAD BUZZ IS TO ADMIT TO IT**. As we all know, admitting your mistakes is a step in the right direction. It's the same with bad buzz. If you address the bad buzz first, then you can get to your good buzz. When you do this, people will be amazed that you know the bad buzz and will usually forgive you. Addressing the bad buzz will build a huge amount of trust with the other person. There's always going to be an answer to bad buzz, but the problem is that most people don't *know* that answer.

When I did my first survey, I realized that I had bad buzz about my high school past. When I started addressing this up front with these agent moms, it made me more trustworthy. Here's how I spun my bad buzz: "Ms. Jones, I know you remember me as a wild and crazy guy from high school, but now I'm serious about the mortgage business, and they call me the straight shooter because I always tell my agents the truth."

You might have been a big drinker and now you aren't. You might have been bad at returning calls, but now you have corrected your ways. When you acknowledge your baggage, you increase your trustworthiness. Politicians and the media call this **SPIN**.

D U M P I N G   Y O U R   B U Z Z

When it comes to dripping buzz, it is important that you do not cross that fine line and start dumping buzz, or unloading all of your buzz at once. Dumping buzz only works in certain settings and scenarios.

If you're at a network meeting and you introduce yourself and your company, you should take advantage and **DUMP BUZZ** all over them. The buzz you're dumping is the same list that you would recite at a Chamber of Commerce meeting: "Hello, I work for Steve at State Farm. Here's what's great about me, here's what's great about Steve, here's what's great about you, here's what's great about State Farm."

There are opportunities for you to lay out the whole laundry list, such as in advertising, communication, or even e-mails. For instance, you could decide that this week, everyone is going to change the bio of their e-mails to mention that State Farm's mutual fund has been one of the top-ten mutual funds in the country for the last ten years, since most of your customers don't know that.

Dumping buzz can be great advertising, but it's important to remember that you cannot dump unless the situation is set up for you to do it. The scenario determines whether you're dumping or not.

CREATING YOUR BUZZ

What if you don't have buzz? If this is the case, then you haven't provided anyone with anything buzzable—either bad or good—to say. **YOU HAVE TO CREATE YOUR BUZZ.**

Start thinking about your backstory, and say, "Here's the reason why I qualify for this." Start by creating your own buzz about why you're qualified for whatever it is you do. Before you started in your current profession, what were the things that you could put on your resume that said, "I'm qualified to do this"? How did you go from being in the banking business to the restaurant business, for instance? The point is, there's a backstory to that.

By describing your backstory and how it brought you to where you are, you're buzzing people on why you're qualified in your profession.

You must spin your qualifications and buzz your assets. A great example is for stay-at-home moms who are ready to get back in the workforce. "You know, I'm really good at organizing," they might say. "I have four kids and I have to organize them every day." "I'm really good at mentoring people. I had to mentor my four children and help them do their homework every day." By looking at your backstory and analyzing your strengths, you can start using those correlations as proof of why you're qualified to do a certain job.

GETTING OTHERS TO BUZZ FOR YOU

My friend Craig called me recently, saying that he needed a chiropractor. He wanted to know the best chiropractor in Alpharetta. In response, I said he needed to see Chris.

"Come on, you need to go see Chris," I said. "Chris is a guy who I would go to. I've sent my daughter to him and she's been happy with what he's done. He's from South Georgia, a good old boy, so he'll charge you fairly."

I was buzzing about him.

I then called Chris and said, "Chris, my buddy Craig is going to come see you. He's a good friend of mine, and his wife is really involved in her school. It will be great for her to know about you—she's sort of a mouthpiece and she'll tell a lot of people about your business. Craig is in the healthcare business; he's got wonderful insurance and an excellent job, so you don't have to worry about getting paid . . ."

I didn't have to call Chris and buzz him about Craig, but it helped to solidify the relationship between them so that when they met, they'd say, "Isn't Beech a great guy?"

I call that **SOCIAL EQUITY**. In this case, I've created social equity between two people who know I went out of my way to help them and give them plenty of information on why this is a good fit, and they know they need to reciprocate sometime. When they're looking for opportunities to reciprocate, they might send some referrals my way.

The best way to get a referral is to give a referral.

I could have said, "Here's Chris's number; see if he can see you today." But I went the extra mile because I know they'll do the same thing for me when the chance comes up. For example, if a customer, friend, or family member comes to them and says, "Hey, I need to refinance and get a mortgage, the whole shebang." They'll say, "You've got to see Beech. Let me call him for you."

The goal is to get *other* people buzzing about you, and the best way to get people to buzz about you is to come up with a catchy, buzzable phrase. Buzzing somebody else can increase your chances of them buzzing you, but the catchier the phrase and more consistent your message is, the more likely you'll see better results and more buzzing. It's like getting referrals, but not entirely the same. I'm not only going to give you the referral; I'm going to give you the extra behind the referral. All they know is that they owe you a referral. If they just gave my name and number to somebody, in their mind they've reciprocated—it doesn't matter if that person ever does business or not. **BUT IF YOU GET THEM TO BUZZ YOU WHEN THEY GIVE THE REFERRAL, NOW YOU'RE TALKING TRUE GOLD!**

Conclusion
NOW BUZZ OFF

There is only one thing in the world worse than being talked about, and that is not being talked about.

—OSCAR WILDE
The Picture of Dorian Gray

Y ou have buzz whether you like it or not. People are going to talk, and they will talk about you and your business. The most important thing to know is that you can have a say in what others are saying! It's all about buzz.

The process is easy. Listen to the way other people introduce you. Does that introduction sound like it could inspire the other person to do business with you? If not, consider doing something different. Ask your spouse and employees what others say about you. Conduct a survey. Gather info on good and bad buzz, then go about changing that buzz to your advantage.

The truth is, most of us can't just think of our buzz, just like we can't think of what our unique selling proposition is. The first step is to discover your unique selling proposition—what it is that makes customers want to use your business—and make that your buzz! Make use of the buzz surveys, and don't forget to have your employees on the same wavelength about what it is that makes your company special. This way, they can effectively communicate the good buzz to your customers, who will, in turn, repeat that buzz to your future customers.

The ultimate goal of all this is to have someone walk up to you and say your buzz right back to you. I will never forget when a stranger walked up to me and said, "Hello, straight shooter!" Your buzz is out there; now it's up to you to find and shape it.

Happy buzzing!

Sample BUZZ SURVEY

Create a list of past customers, friends, current customers, and potential people you don't know who should be using your business. Hire a friend to call the list and ask them the following questions.

The format for your questions should go as follows:

(a) Basic question

(b) Follow-up question

(c) Drip in good buzz to give the person something to think and talk about

Example:

(a) Have you ever heard of Steve Beecham? *(Write down what they say verbatim.)*

(b) How did you meet Steve or first hear about Home Town Mortgage?

(Now, buzz them with something unique or special about you or your business.) Did you know that Steve rode his dirt bike across the continental US, staying 80 percent on dirt roads, from the Atlantic to the Pacific?

Sample SURVEY QUESTIONS

We are doing an informational survey on [*name of individual or business*] to help them determine what they are doing right and what they may want to consider changing.

① a. Have you ever heard of _____? If so, how did

you hear about them?

b. Are you familiar with _____? If so, how do you

know them?

c. Did you know that [*insert buzzworthy fact about*

person and/or business]?

② a. Have you ever done business with _____?

b. How did they do? If you were displeased, why?

c. Did you know that [*insert buzzworthy fact about*

person and/or business]?

③ a. What was your opinion of _____'s business?

b. How could _____ improve your outlook on

their business?

c. Did you know that [*insert buzzworthy fact about person and/or business*]?

4 a. What are the good qualities about [*person/ business*]?

b. What are the bad qualities about [*person/ business*]?

c. Did you know that [*insert buzzworthy fact about person and/or business*]?

5 a. Have you told others about [*person/business*]?

b. Would you refer others to use [*person/business*]? Why or why not?

c. Did you know that [*insert buzzworthy fact about person and/or business*]?

6 a. What should [*person/business*] improve upon?

b. What would make it more likely for you to recommend [*person/business*] to friends and family?

c. Did you know that [*insert interesting fact about person/business*]?

If asked directly, what would you tell others about [*person/business*]?

It's vital to follow-up your participants' responses with buzzworthy facts about you or your business. If you skip this important step, you're missing out on the perfect opportunity to drip buzz, which could improve your business in the long run. Dripping buzz in this way is not bragging, but naturally cluing them in on something they may not know during the course of the conversation.

Endnotes

1. Jacques Bughin, Jonathan Doogan, Ole Jorgen Vetvik, "A New Way to Measure Word-of-Mouth Marketing," *McKinsey Quarterly*, http://www.mckinsey.com/business-functions/marketing-and-sales/our-insights/a-new-way-to-measure-word-of-mouth-marketing.

2. Imani Mixon, "40 Word-of-Mouth Marketing Statistics That You Should Know," *Ambassador*, December 30, 2015, https://www.getambassador.com/blog/word-of-mouth-marketing-statistics.

3. David Saad, Dr., "Viral Marketing Best Practices by Calibra," Calibra, January 15, 2013, http://www.slideshare.net/Luristic/viral-marketing-best-practices.

4. "Arbitron Study Finds More Than Half of Frequent Moviegoers Find Commercials Before Movies More Acceptable than Commercials on TV," BusinessWire, March 08, 2007, http://www.businesswire.com/news/home/20070308005822/en/Arbitron-Study-Finds-Frequent-Moviegoers-Find-Commercials.

5. "Seven in 10 Americans Seek out Opinions before Making Purchases," Mintel, June 3, 2015, http://www.mintel.com/press-centre/social-and-lifestyle/seven-in-10-americans-seek-out-opinions-before-making-purchases.

6. "The Urge to Gossip," Emotional Detective, February 16, 2012, http://emotionaldetective.typepad.com/emotional-detective/2012/02/gossip.html.

7. Roy H. Williams, *The Wizard of Ads: Turning Words Into Magic and Dreamers Into Millionaires* (Austin, TX: Bard Press, 1998).

Also by
STEVE BEECHAM

Available at
bassackwardbusiness.com

Contact the Author
Steve Beecham
beech@stevebeecham.com
(770) 634-2531
65 Roswell Street, Suite 500
Alpharetta, GA 30009

About
THE AUTHOR

Steve Beecham is the "Straight Shooter" of the mortgage business in Atlanta. As a successful businessman and entrepreneur, he has spent many years looking for the perfect scenario: "My phone rings, and they ask me how to spend money with me."

He has owned a retail store, a mortgage company, a garbage business, and rental real-estate properties. Steve is the past president of the Georgia Association of Mortgage Brokers and has been listed as one of the top-five mortgage companies in the state of Georgia by the *Atlanta Business Chronicle*. He has served on numerous nonprofit boards and has led the way in innovative marketing ideas for them to grow their business. As president of Home Town Mortgage, he has taught his buzzable strategies to his team and other companies.

Steve coaches and speaks to companies like Edward Jones, Wells Fargo, John Hancock, Merrill Lynch, Prudential, Aflac, Allstate, State Farm, Nationwide Insurance, COUNTRY Financial, Savannah College of Art and Design, University of Georgia, and Georgia State University.

Find out more and sign up for a free newsletter at bassackwardbusiness.com.